My First Transportation Books

PLANES GO!

Harold Morris

TABLE OF CONTENTS

A Crabtree Seedlings Book

Planes

Passenger planes take off from airports.

They fly high above the clouds.

etwork
Airline
Management
ADC

Cargo planes carry goods.

They can carry heavy loads.

5т
GLDU 323950 9
22G1
MGW.
TARE.
NET.
CU.CAP.
Volga-Dnepr
Volga-Dnepr
К766КК 94

Super scoopers are planes that drop water on forest fires.

They scoop the water from nearby lakes.

The F-15EX is a fighter jet.

OT
53 WG
002

OT
53 WG
002

It is used by the **U.S. Air Force.**

CHRONO
SIDE STICK PRIORITY
Std
CSTR
WPT
VOR.D
NDB
ARPT
MACH
HDG
LAT
ROSE
NAV
ARC
PLAN
ADF
VOR
OFF
FD
LS
SPD
MACH
LOC
PFD
PFD/ND XFR
ND
LOUD SPEAKER
CONSOLE/FLOOR
MACH
ALT CRZ
NAV
AP2
1 FD 2
A/THR
ALMIK 337°
VOR1
DGP
VOR2
DGP
TERR ON ND
ENG
AIR
PEDALS
ACTIVE
STBY/CRS
VHF1
VHF2
VHF3
LOAD

All planes have a cockpit.

A **pilot** sits in the cockpit and makes the plane go!

Glossary

passenger (PASS-uhn-jur): A passenger is someone who travels in a plane or other vehicle and is not the driver or pilot.

pilot (KROOZ): A pilot is someone who flies a plane.

planes (PLANEZ): Planes are machines with wings that fly through the air. The word planes is short for airplanes.

U.S. Air Force (YOO ESS AIR FORSS): The U.S. Air Force is the part of the United States fighting forces that fights from the air.

Index

School-to-Home Support for Caregivers and Teachers

This book helps children grow by letting them practice reading. Here are a few guiding questions to help the reader build his or her comprehension skills. Possible answers appear here in red.

Before Reading

- **What do I think this book is about?** I think this book is about how fast planes can go. I think this book is about different types of planes.
- **What do I want to learn about this topic?** I want to learn if a plane can take me to the North Pole. I want to learn if I must go to school to learn how to fly a plane.

During Reading

- **I wonder why...** I wonder why a plane flys high above the clouds. I wonder why cargo planes have doors in the front and in the back.
- **What have I learned so far?** I have learned that super scoopers are planes that drop water on forest fires. I have learned that all planes have a cockpit.

After Reading

- **What details did I learn about this topic?** I have learned that super scoopers scoop the water from lakes to help put fires out. I have learned that the F-15EX is a fighter jet used by the U.S. Air Force.
- **Read the book again and look for the glossary words.** I see the word *passenger* on page 2, and the word *pilot* on page 21. The other glossary words are found on pages 22 and 23.

Library and Archives Canada Cataloguing in Publication

Available at the Library and Archives Canada

Library of Congress Cataloging-in-Publication Data

Available at the Library of Congress

Crabtree Publishing Company

www.crabtreebooks.com 1–800–387–7650

Print book version produced jointly with Blue Door Education in 2023

Written by: Harold Morris

Print coordinator: Katherine Berti

Printed in the U.S.A./072022/CG20220201

PHOTO CREDITS:

Cover photo © Denis Belitsky, Pages 2-3 © Simlinger, page 4 © ILYA AKINSHIN, page 5 © Jag_cz, pages 6-7 © schusterbauer.com, page 8 © Sanchai Khudpin, page 9 © vicspacewalker, pages 10-11 © Marco Barone, page 12 © Igor Karasi, Page 13 © Roberto Chiartano, page 18-19 © Mikko Ryynanen, page 20 © Hananeko_Studio, page 21 © Natalia Bostan, page 22 top photo © Matej Kastelic. All images from Shutterstock.com except page 14 Courtesy of U.S. Air Force (photo by Samuel King Jr.) and pages 15-17 courtesy of U.S Air Force (photo by 1st Lt Savanah Bray)

Published in the United States
Crabtree Publishing
347 Fifth Ave.
Suite 1402-145
New York, NY 10016

Published in Canada
Crabtree Publishing
616 Welland Ave.
St. Catharines, Ontario
L2M 5V6